25 COLORING PAGES

CLASSIC CARS
COLORING
BOOK

FOR KIDS AND ADULTS

SCAN THE QR CODE !

VISIT OUR AUTHOR PAGE ON AMAZON.COM AND CHECK OTHER COLORING PAGES!

Scan Me!

By Juliana Rentell

THIS BOOK BELONGS TO

_____

_____

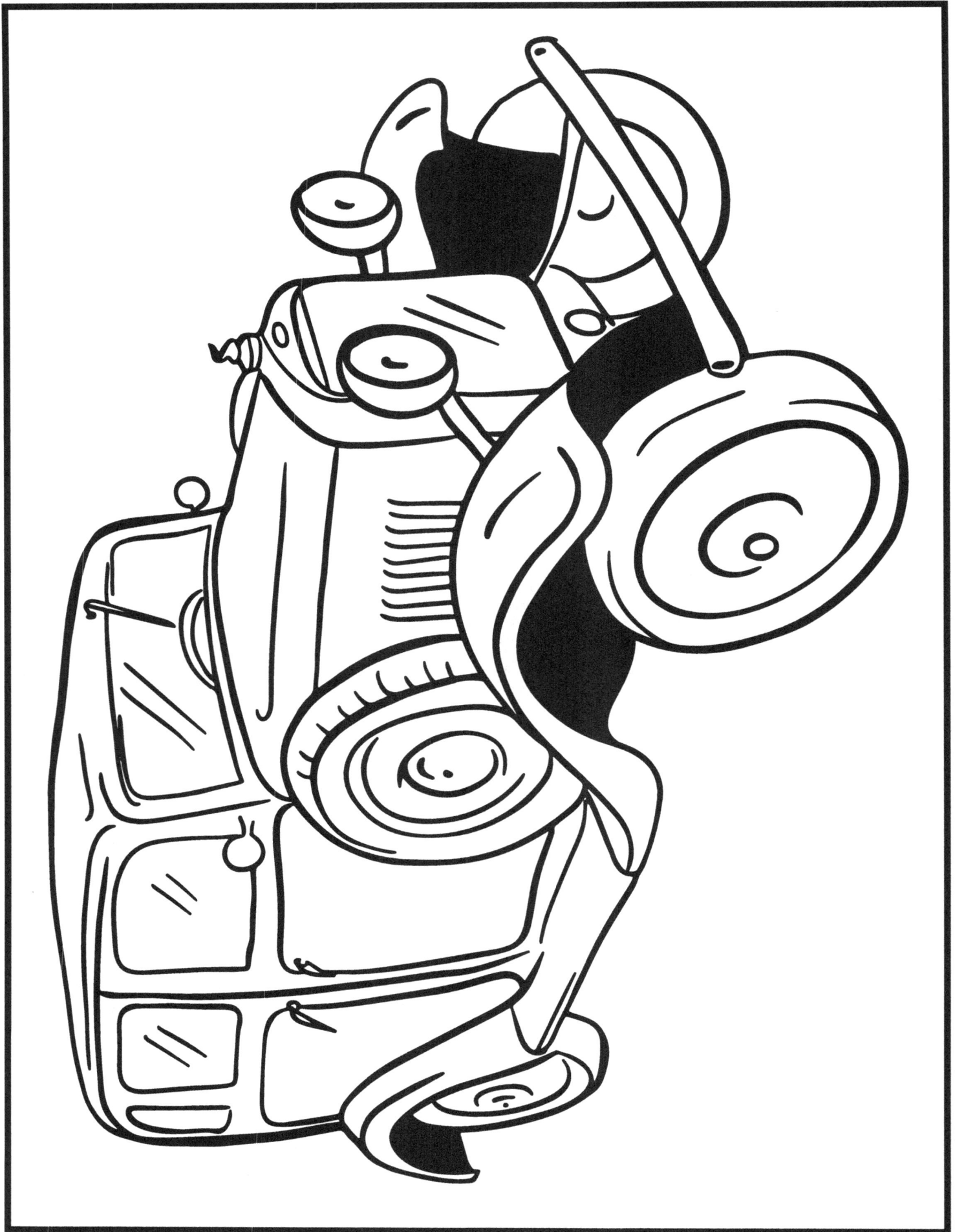

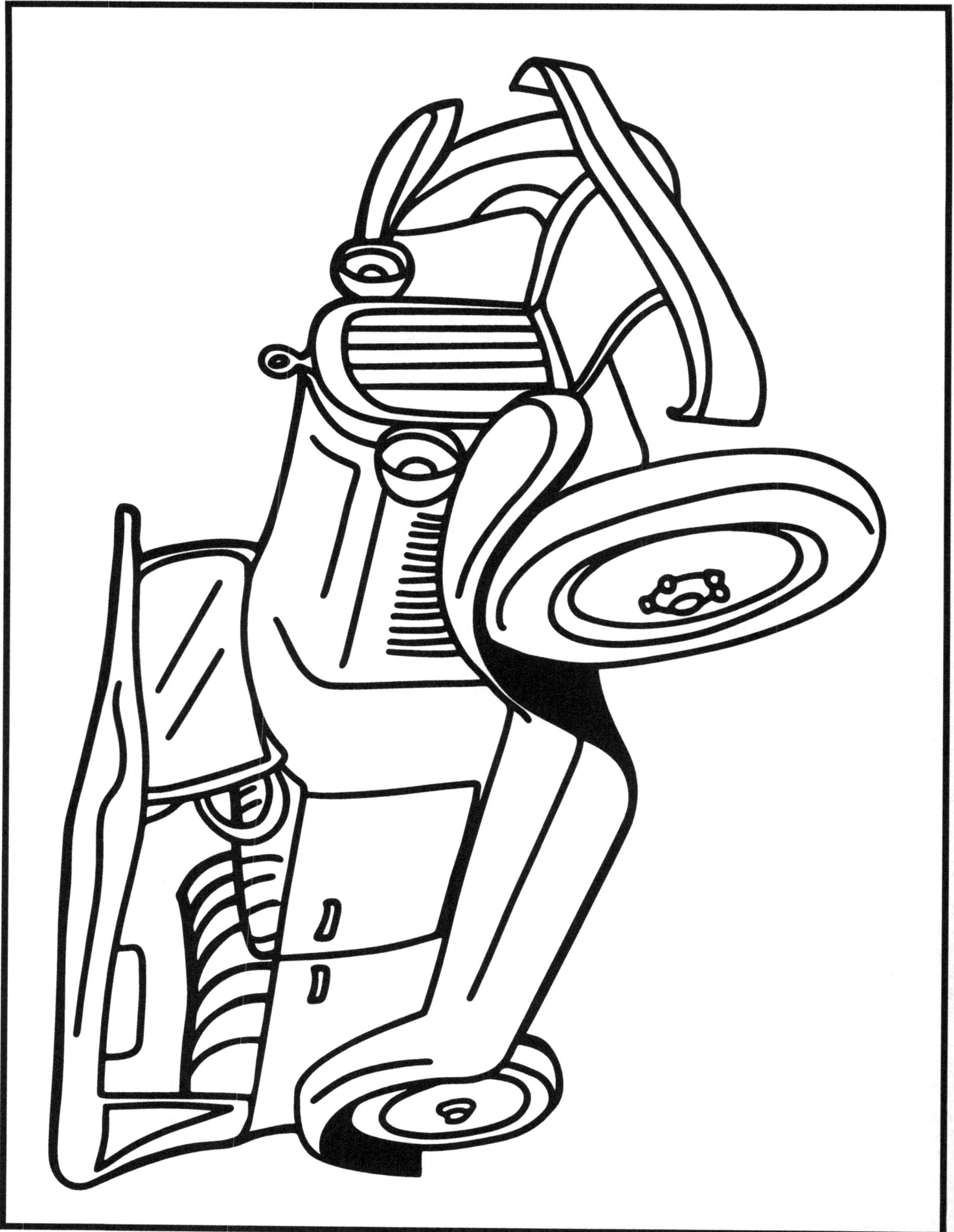

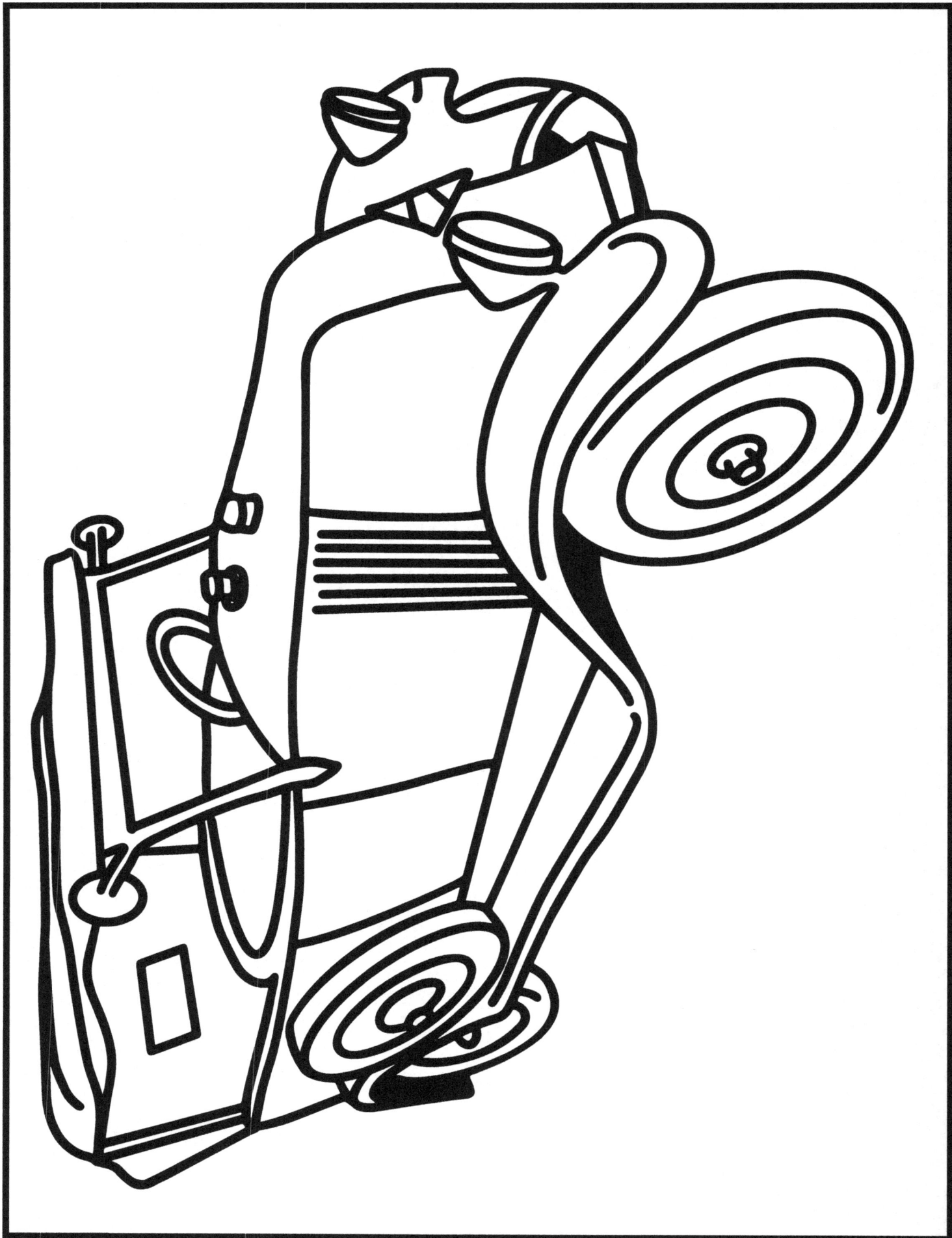

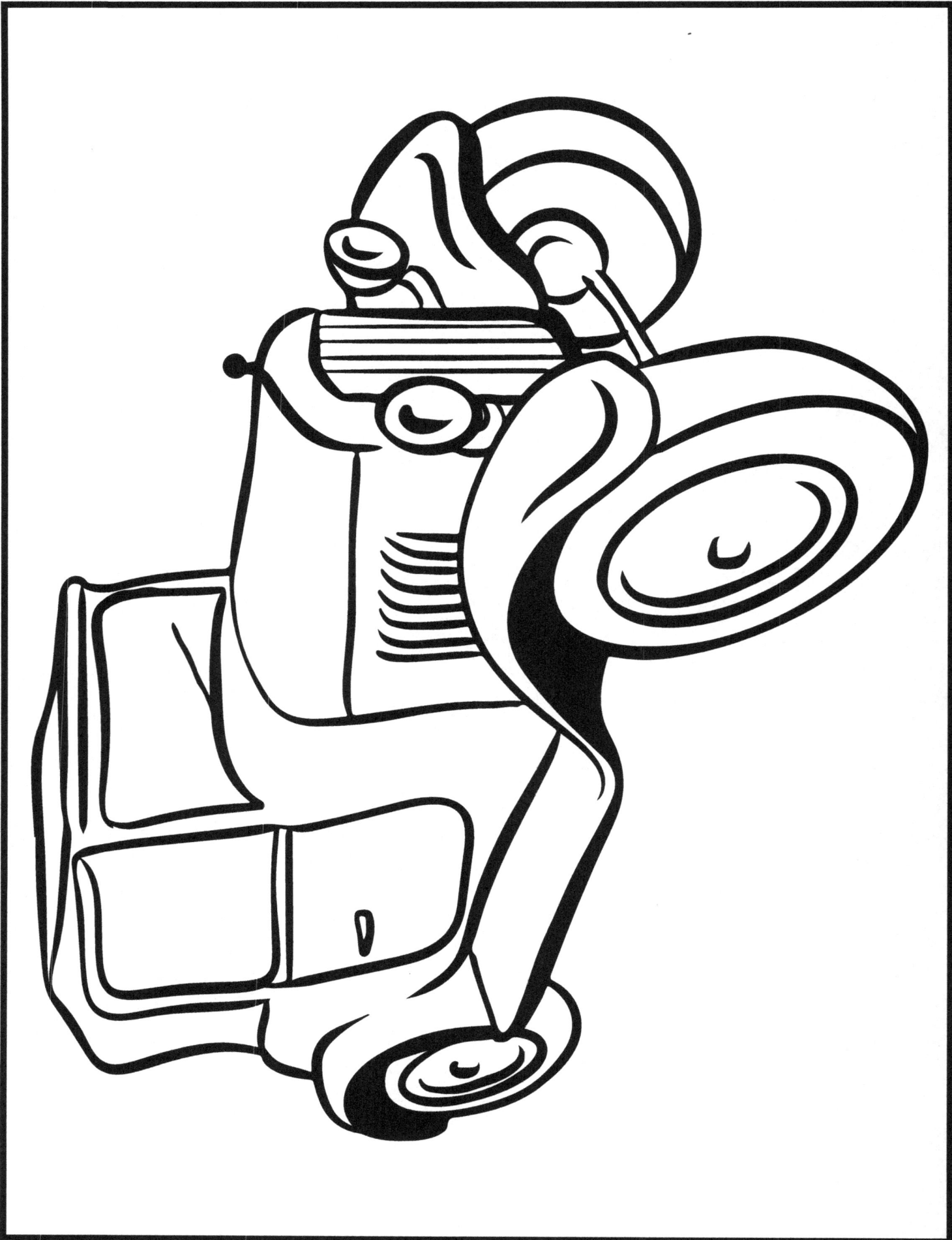

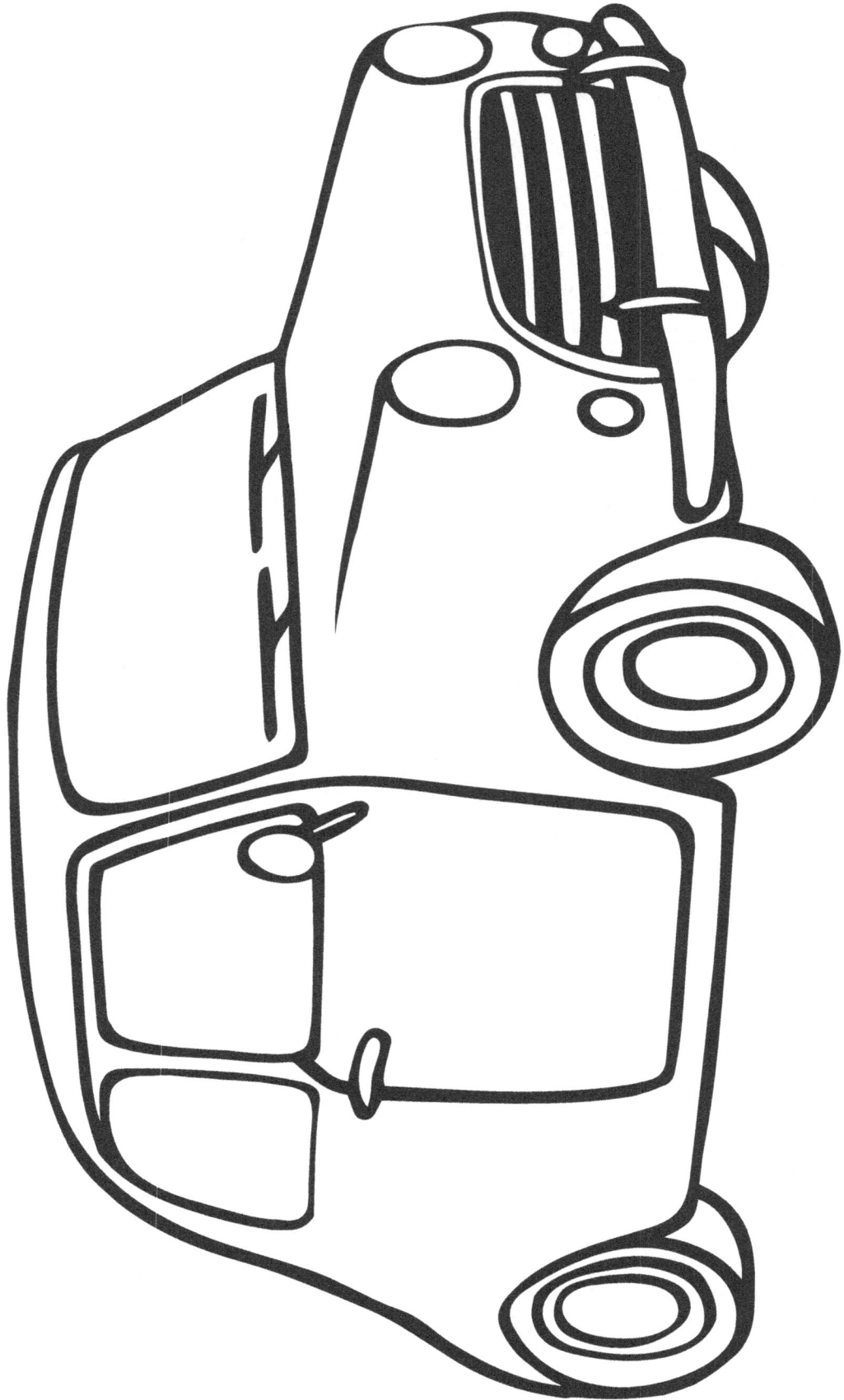

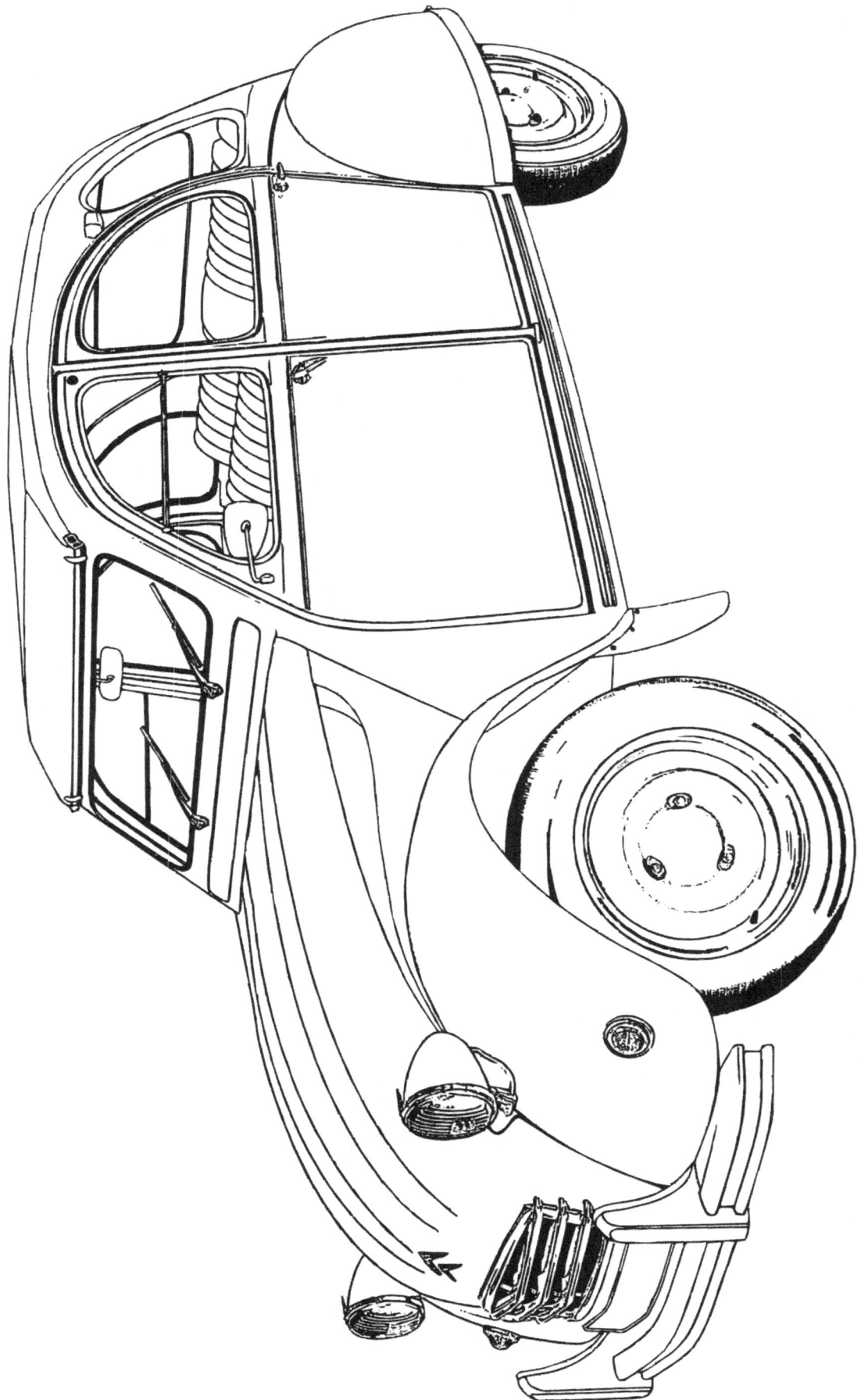

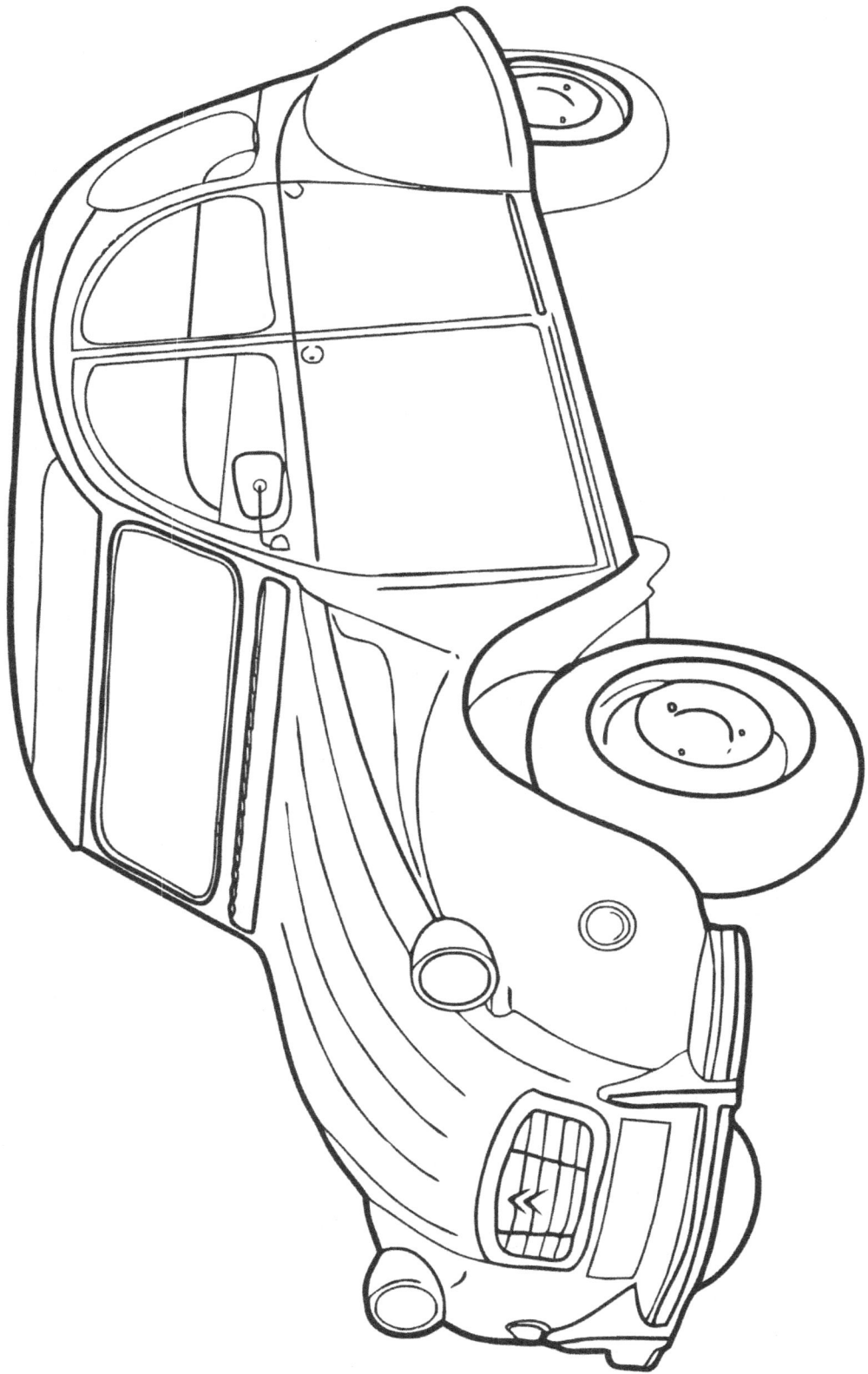

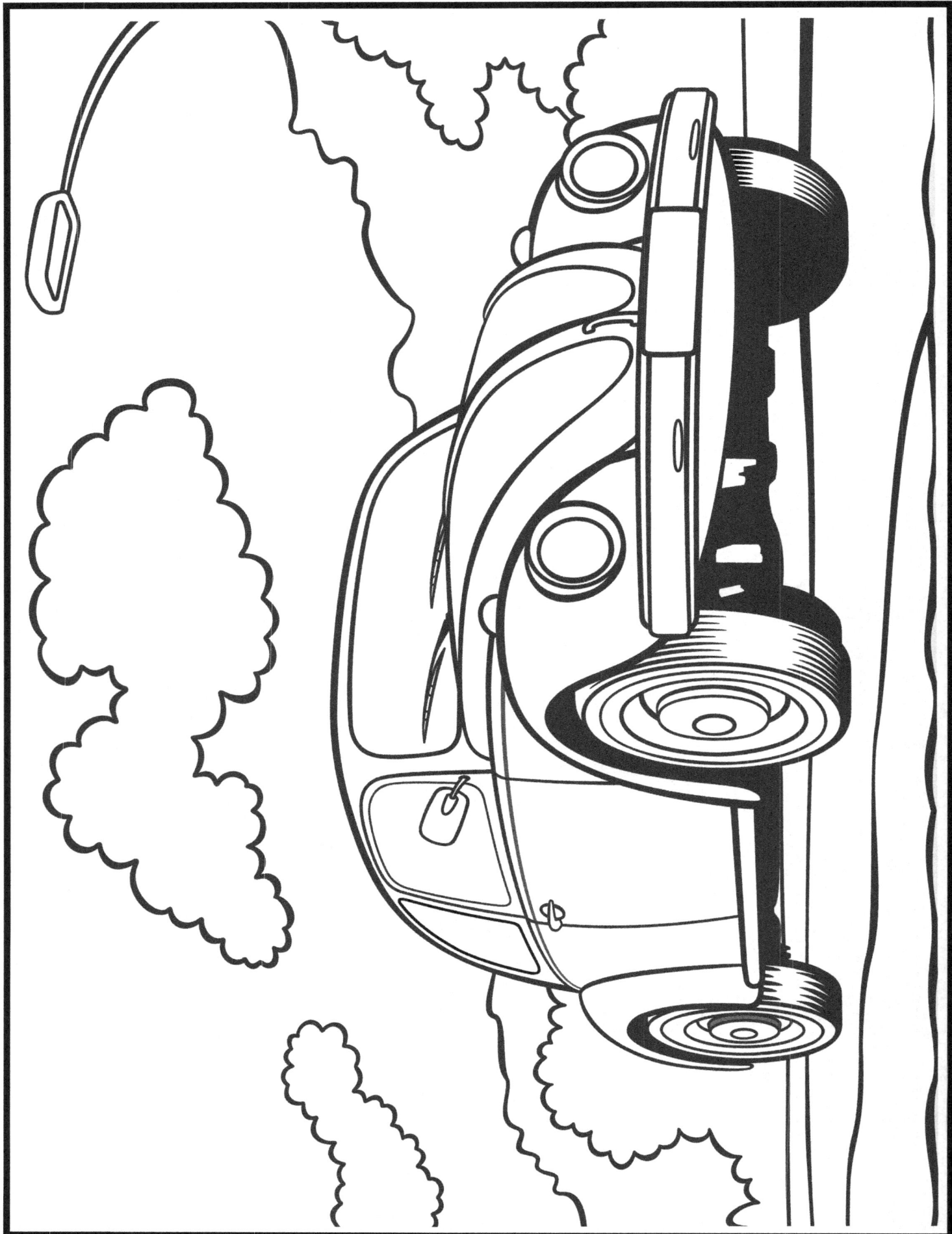

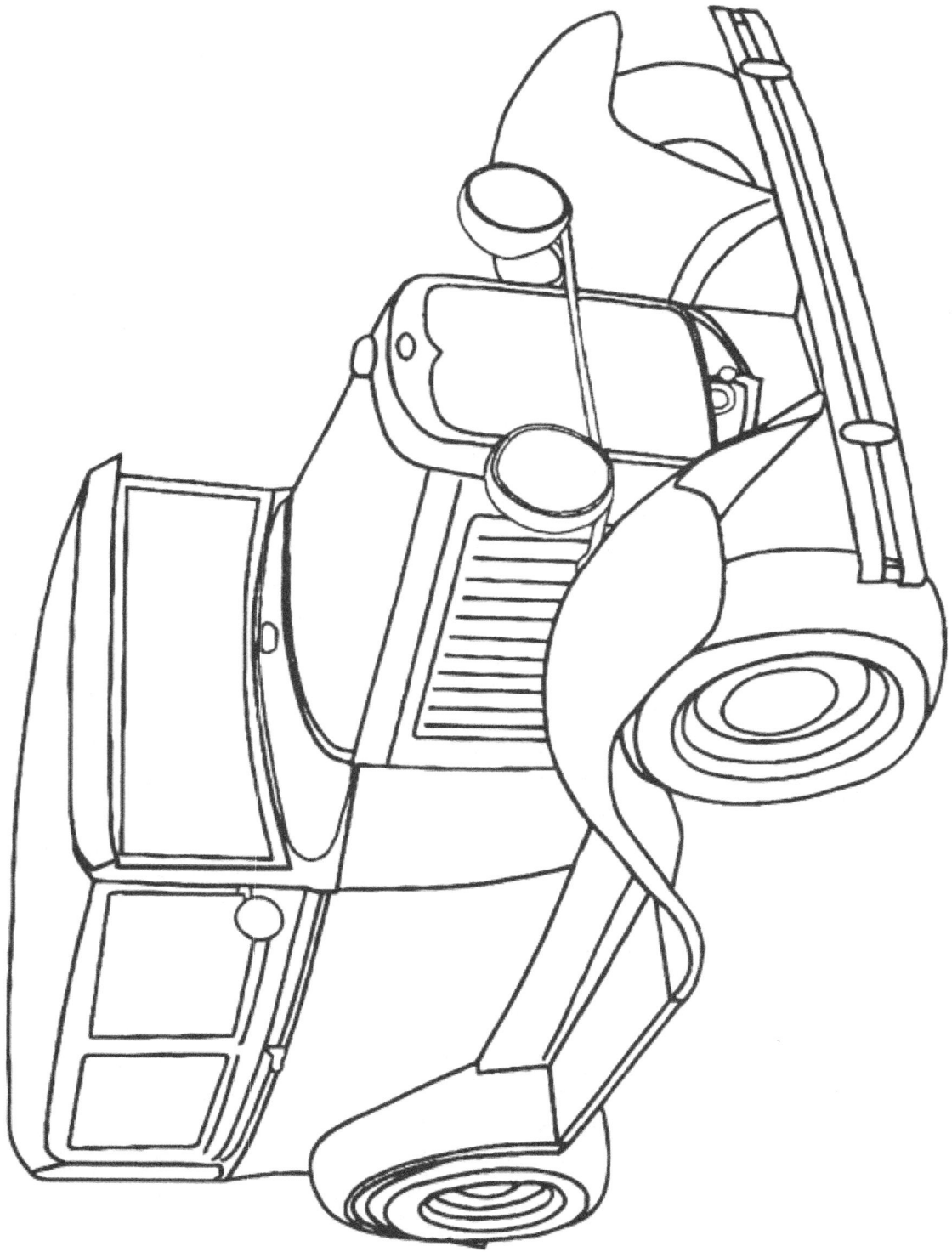

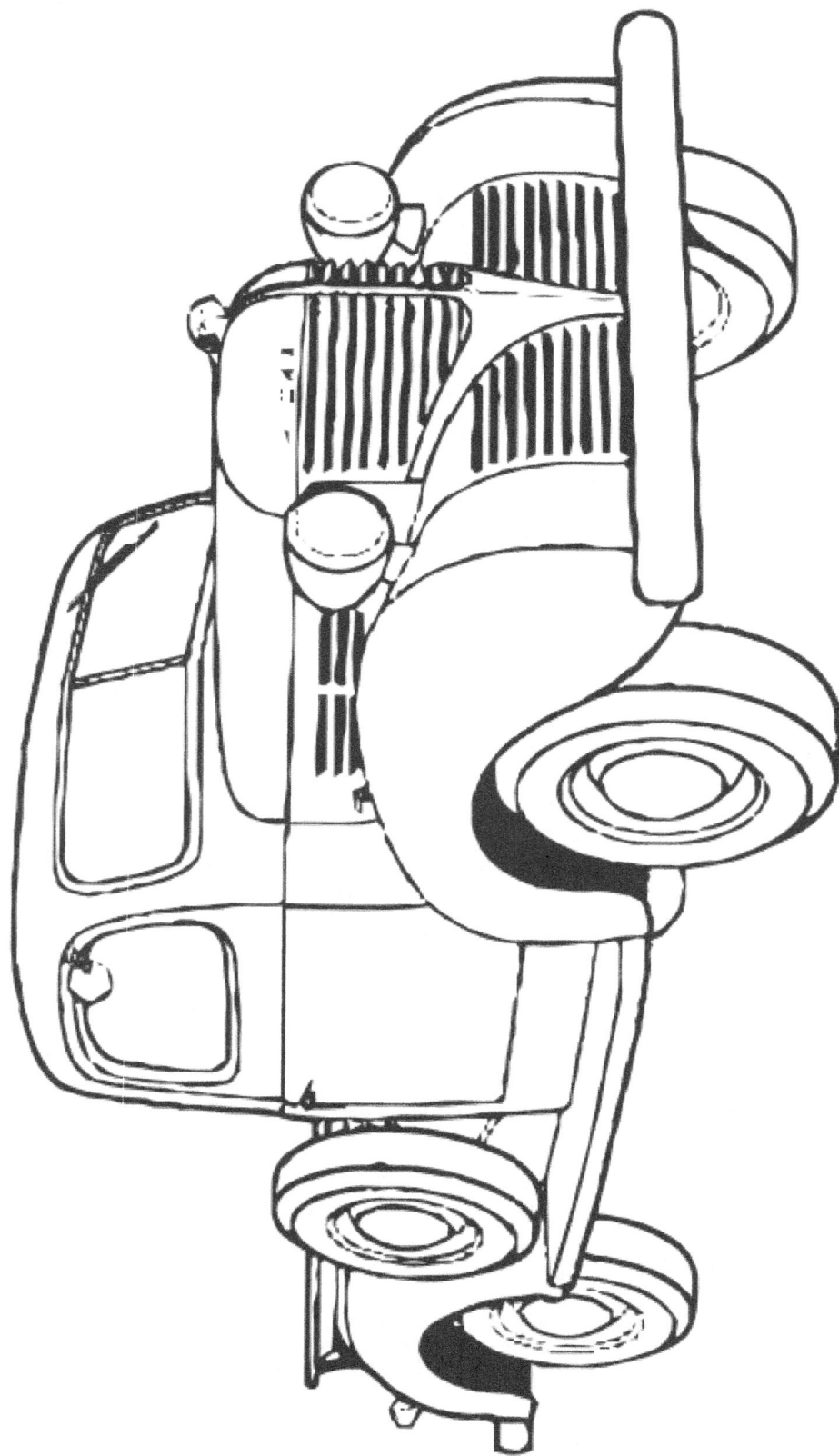

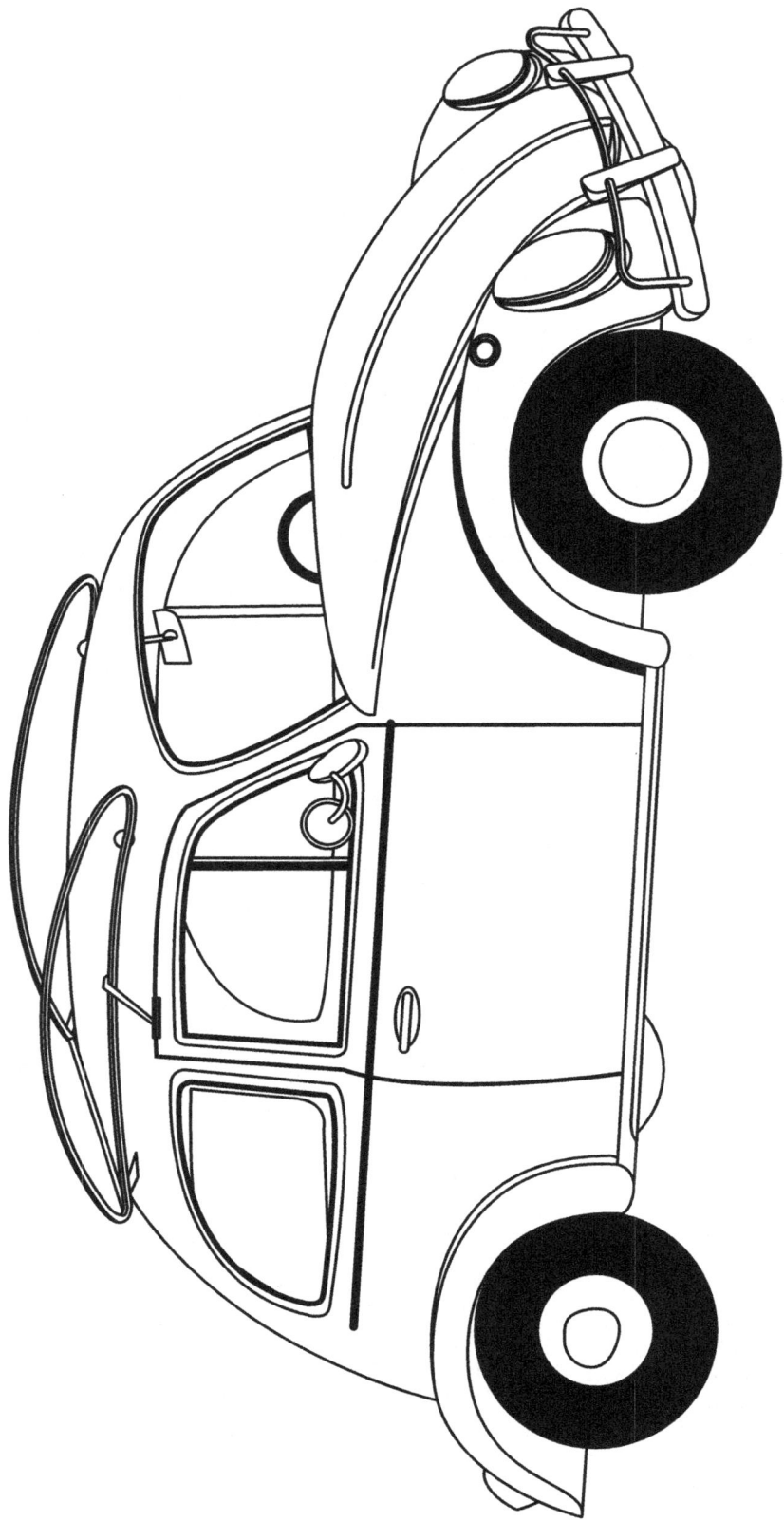

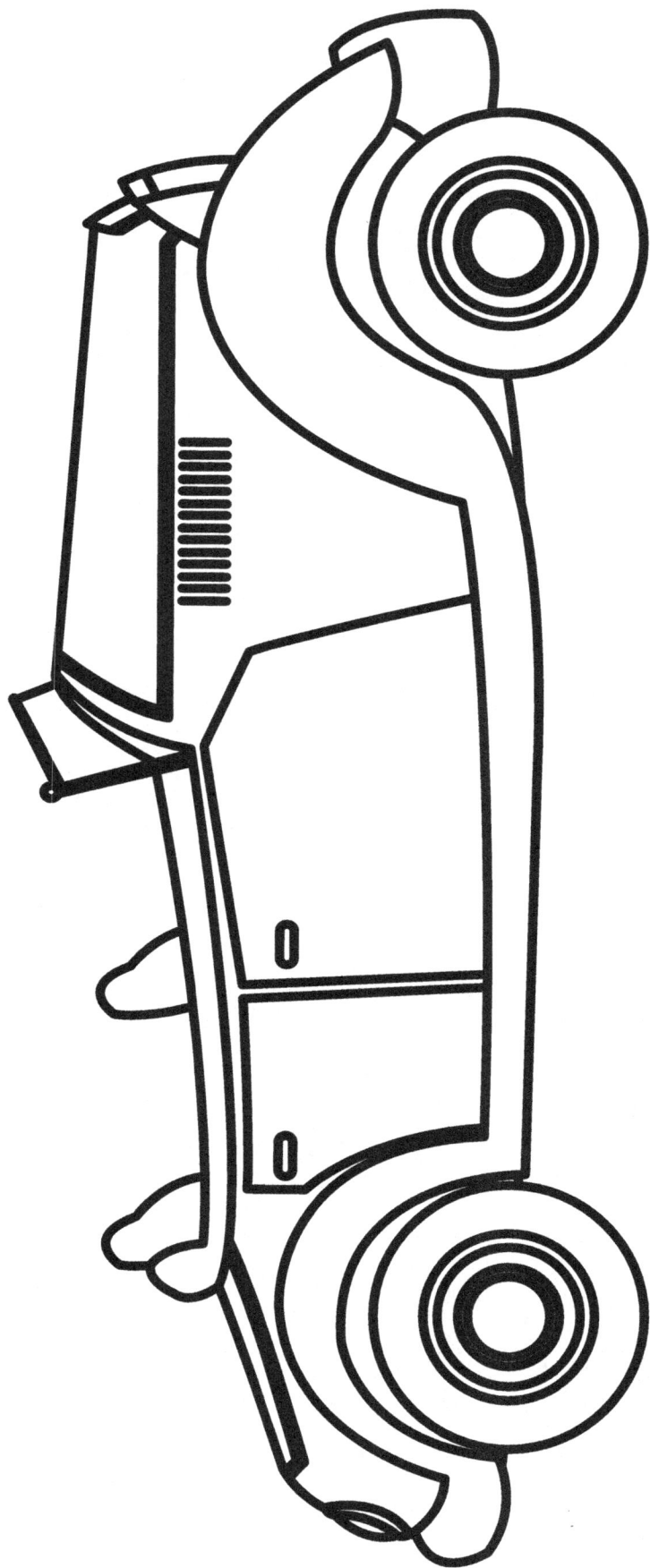

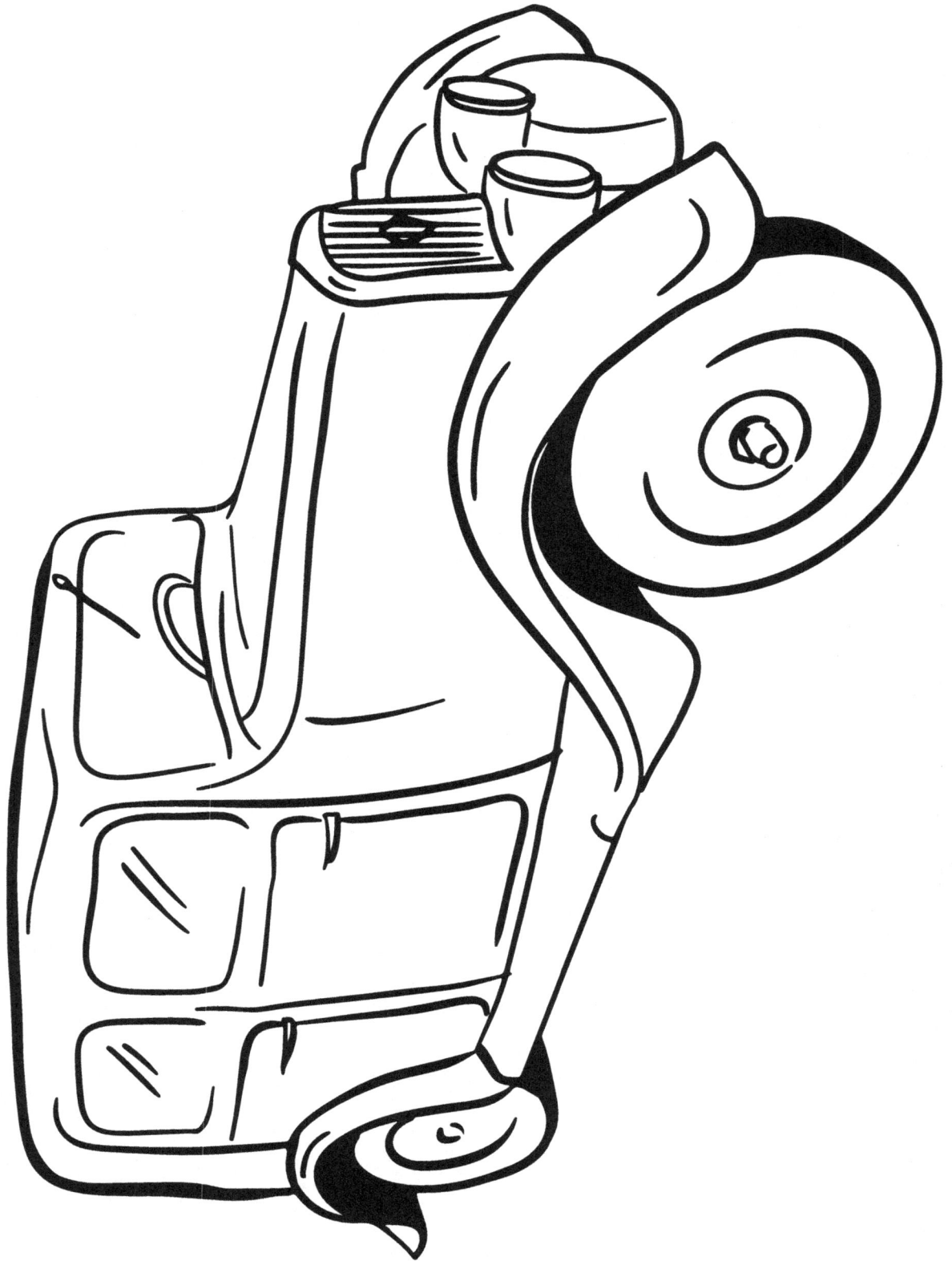

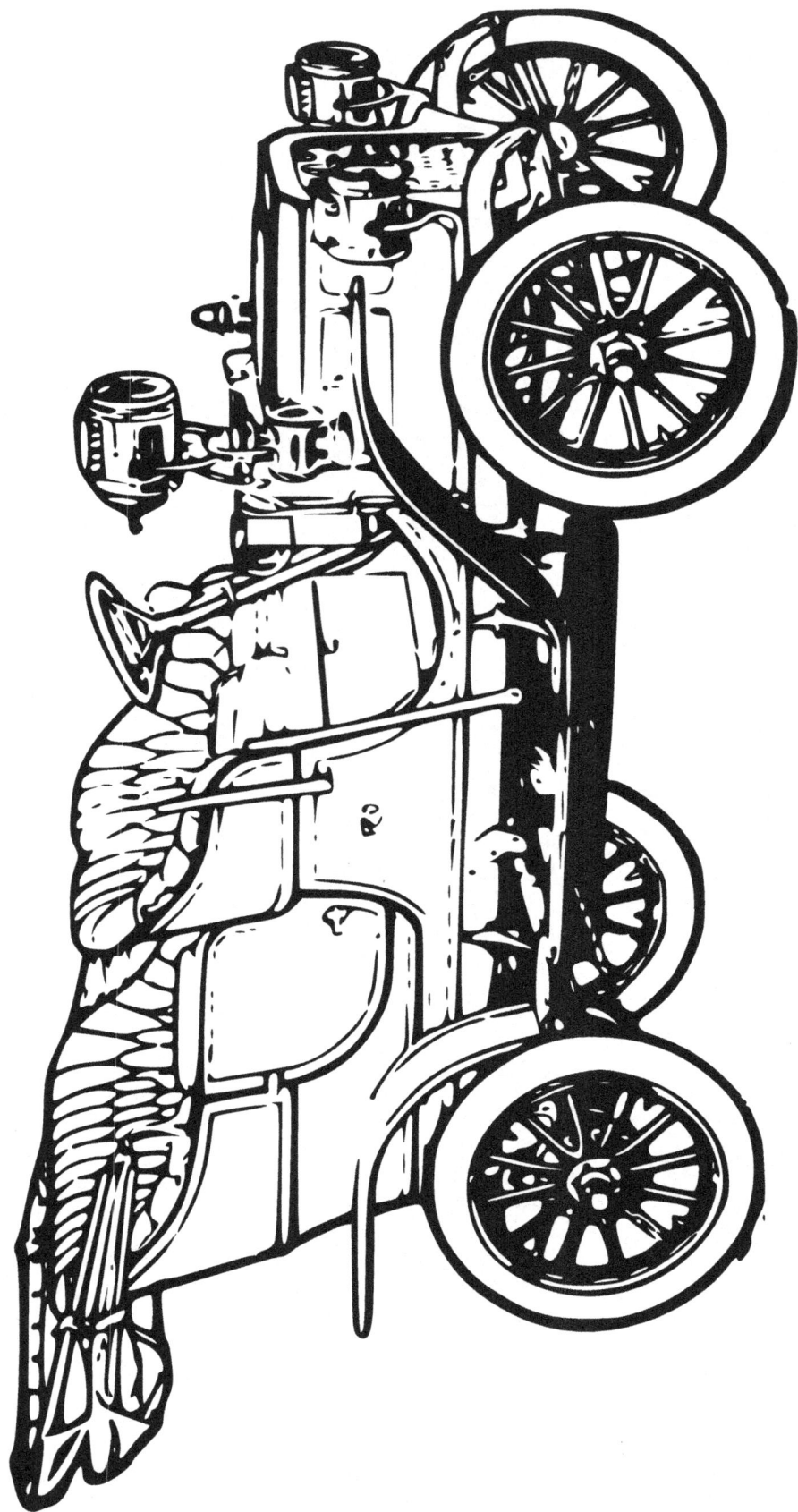

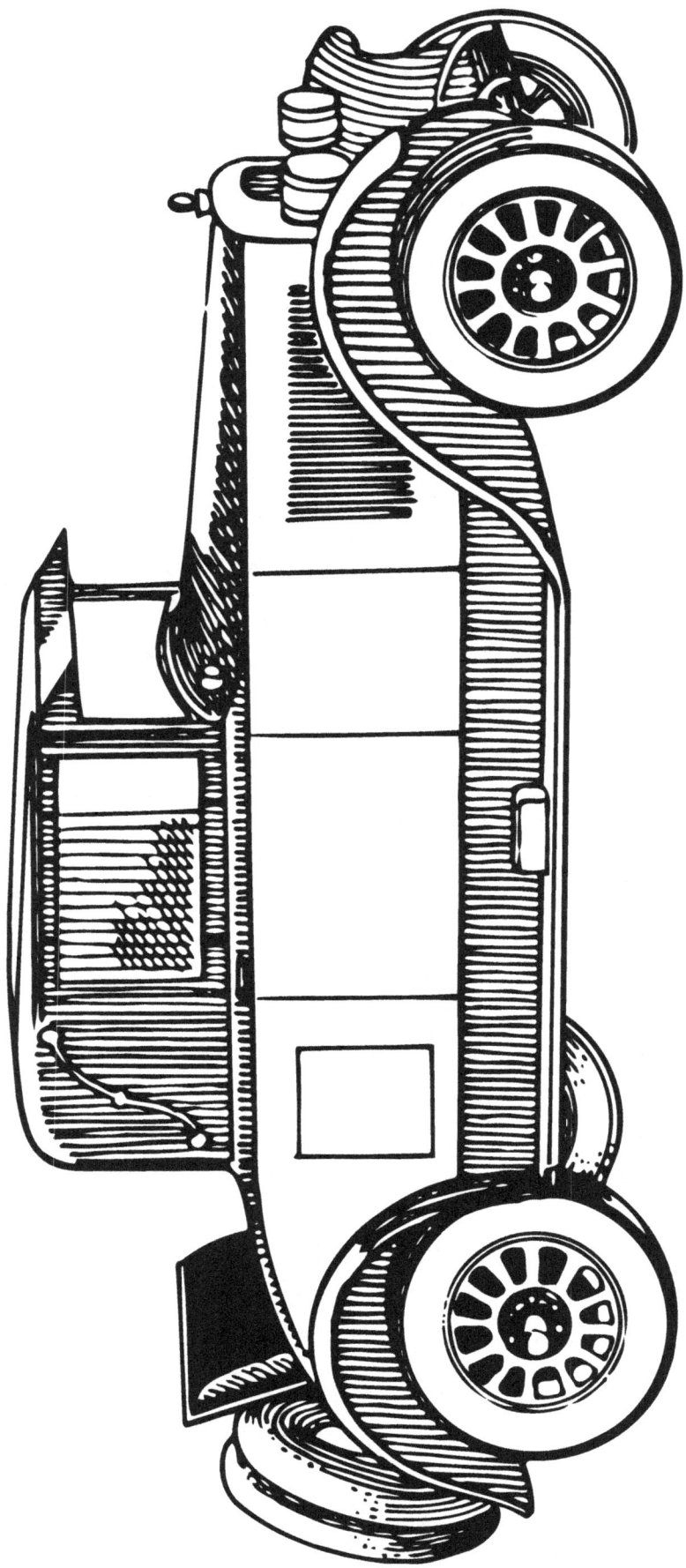

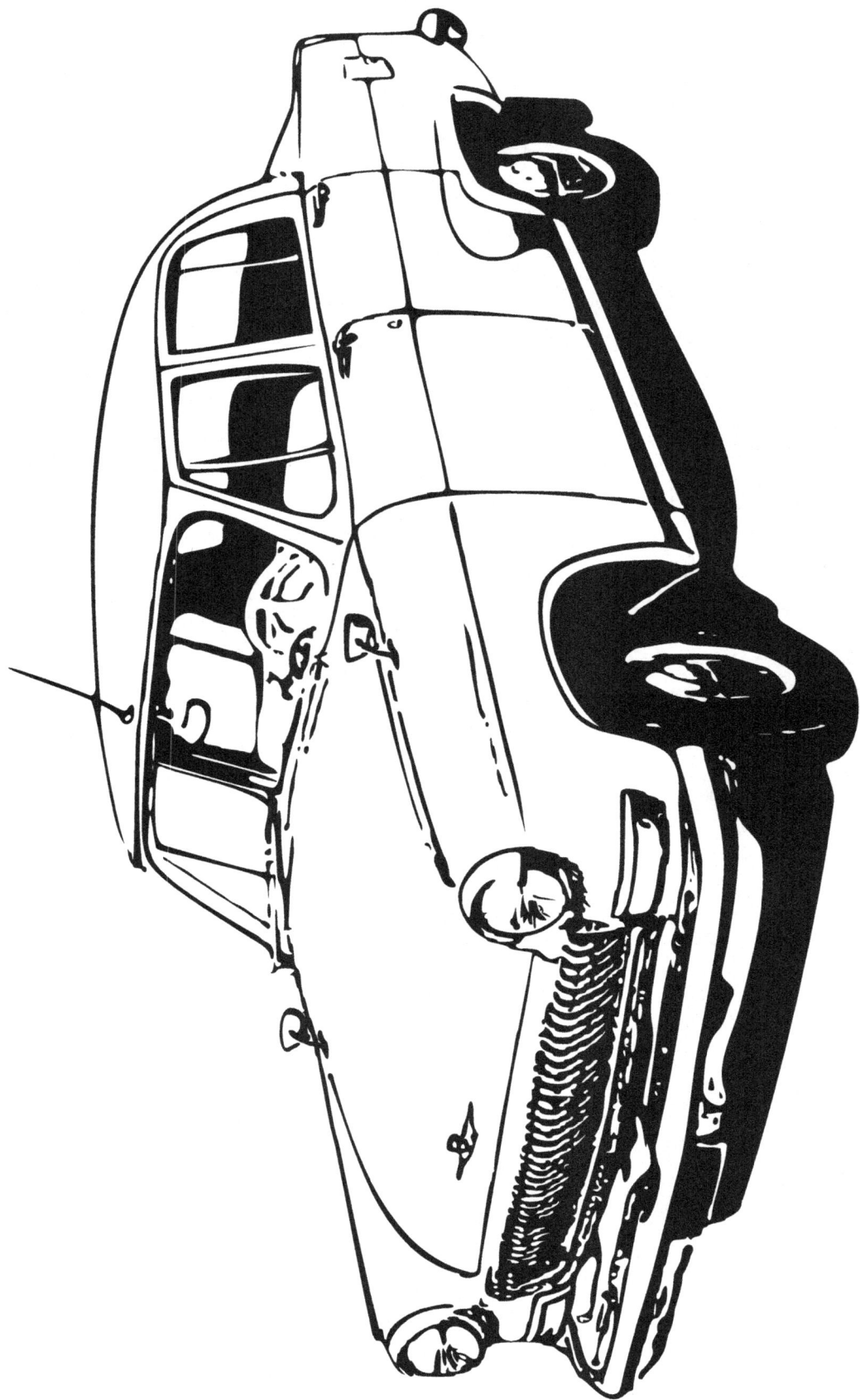

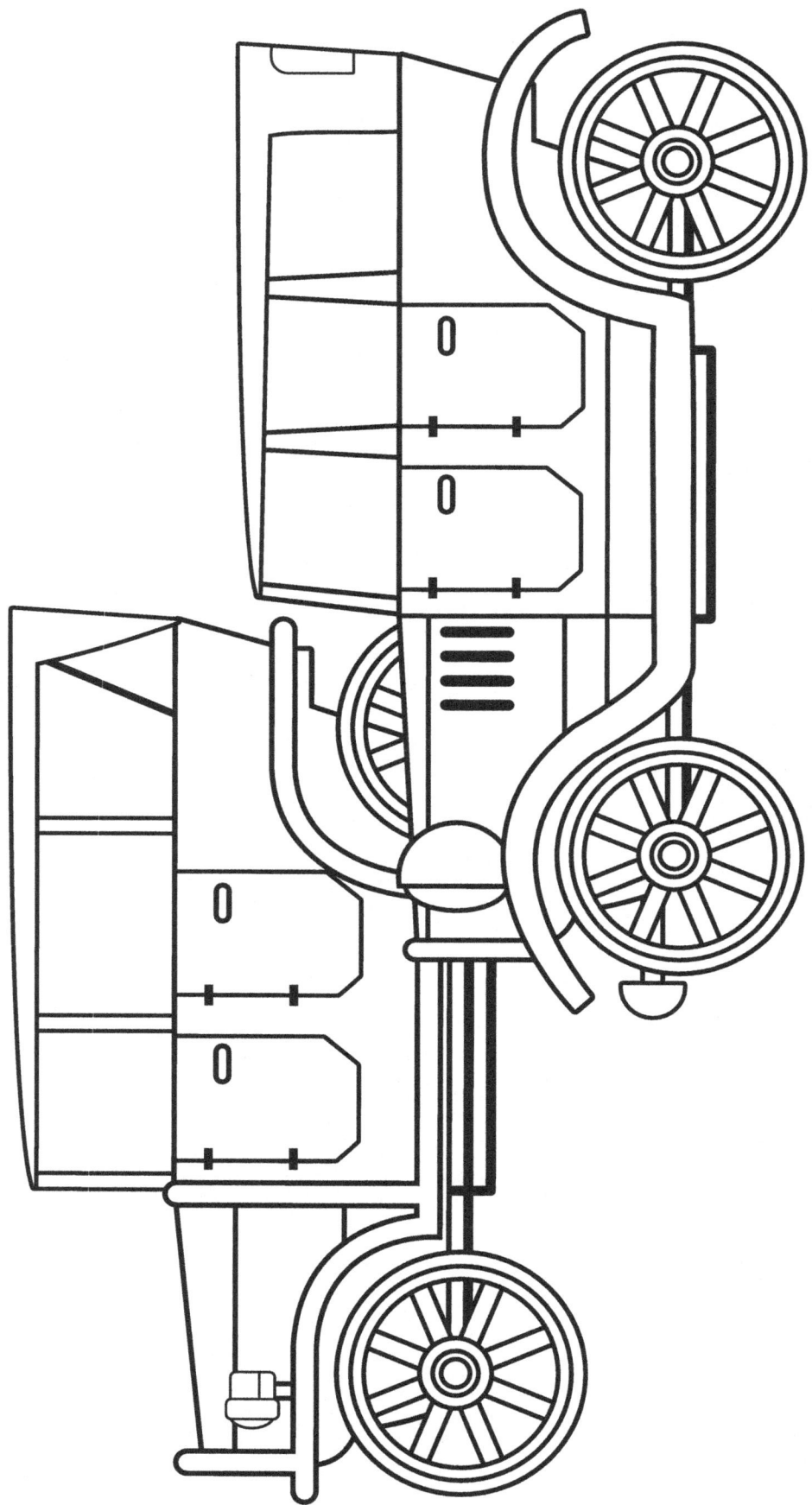

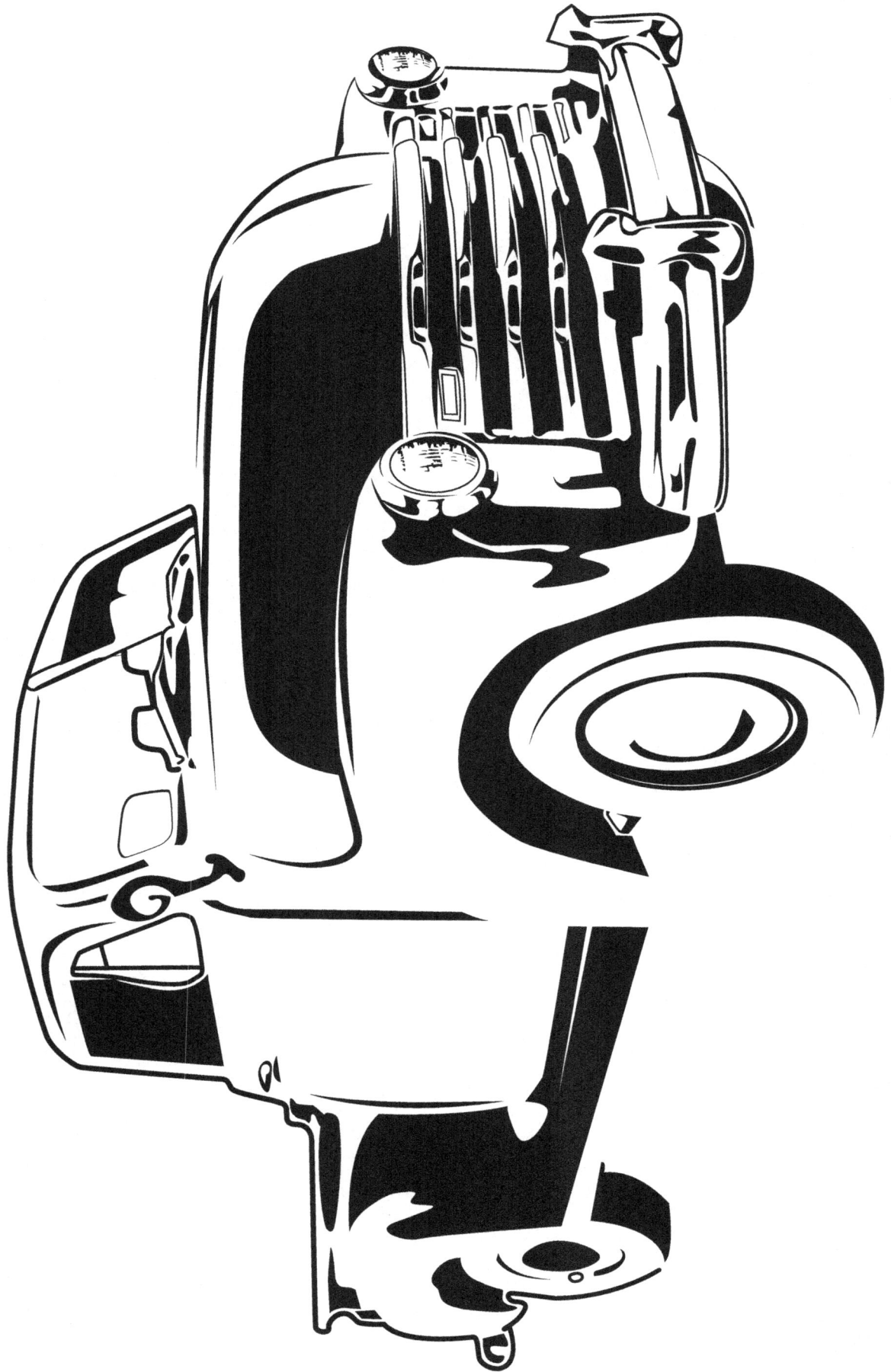

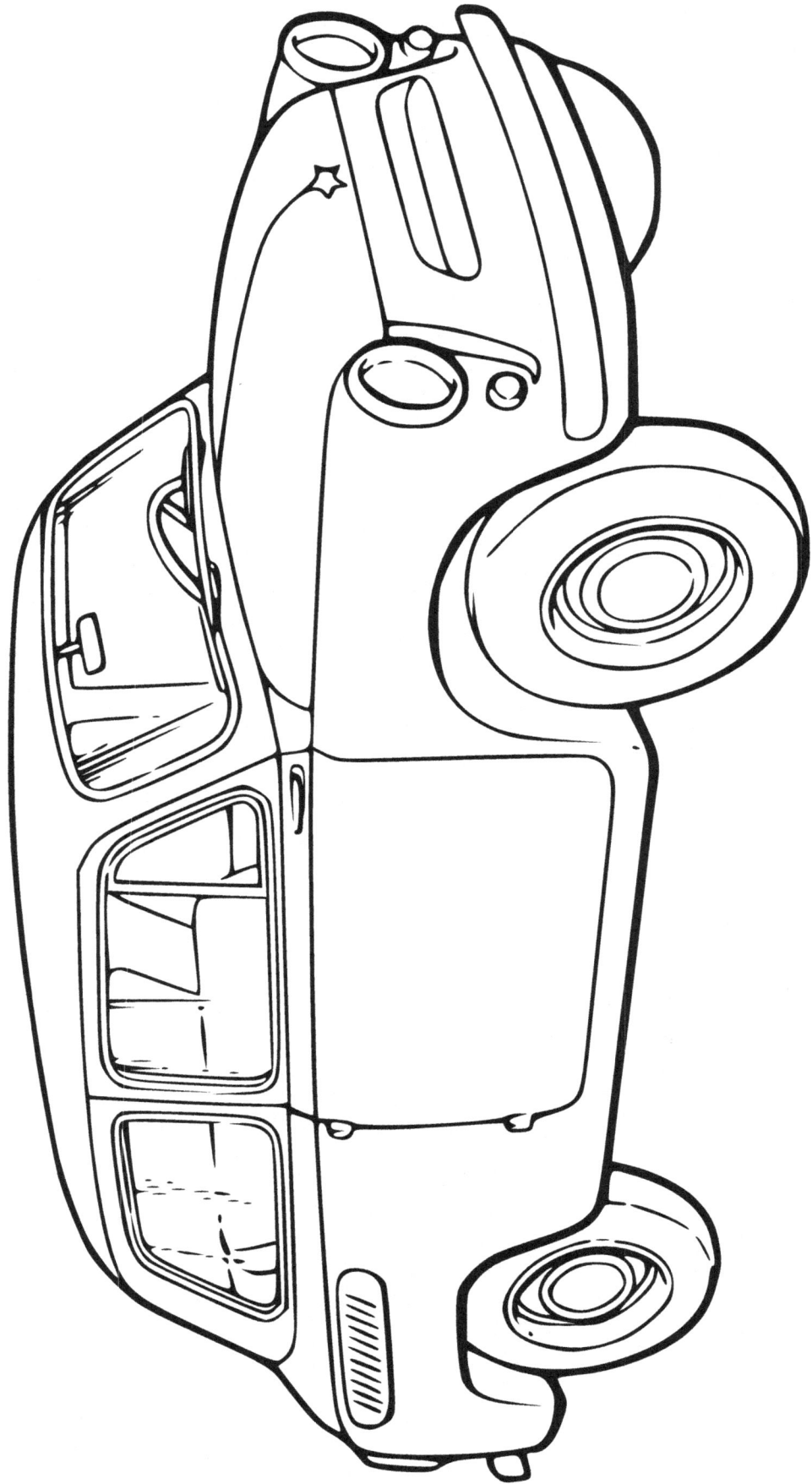

We ask a favor of you

Please leave a review at the Amazon website you bought
this book from.We would really appreciate it.
Keep an eye out for more fun coloring books coming soon

Made in the USA
Las Vegas, NV
16 June 2021